MUM MOMENTS

Journey Through Grief

Copyright © 2014 Judy Taylor

All rights reserved. This book or any portion thereof may not be reproduced or used in any manner whatsoever without the express written permission of the publisher except for the use of brief quotations in a book review or scholarly journal.

First Published by Positive Signs 2014
www.positivesigns.com.au
posigns@bigpond.net.au

Author: Judy Taylor
Cover & Layout: John Taylor

Grateful acknowledgement is made to my father, Ray Martin, for permission to include my Mum's poem on page 5.

Judy Taylor has asserted her right under the Copyright, Designs and Patents Act 1988 to be identified as the author of this work. The information in this book is based on the author's experiences and opinions. The publisher specifically disclaims reponsibility for any adverse consequences which may result from use of the information contained herein.

Printed in Australia by McPherson's Printing Group

ISBN: 978-0-9924900-0-3

Ordering Information:
Special discounts are available on quantity purchases by corporations, associations, educators, and others.
For details contact the publisher at the above email address.

MUM MOMENTS

Journey Through Grief

By Judy Taylor

This journal was inspired by the Love of my Mother

I am so grateful to my mum ...

She gave me the wings to fly

The landscape of my life is changing vastly.

Questions that I may have asked at another time now seem irrelevant.

I do not need to know the route I may take or the destination.

It's enough; however small the experience may seem,
It leads to the unfolding of a new contentment.

I want to sing like a bird for the joy of a new day,
Spread my wings and fly, returning to my nest at night.

I'm deeply connected to those I love, and free to roam as I please.

Life is sweet as we share together.
Life is more beautiful because you are in the world.

Shirley Martin

(A poem by my Mum)

The Dance of Life

My mother has been encouraging me to dance for years. For her the freedom of dance was something she felt I would benefit from as I lived my day to day life.

Dancing to my husband's band with my mum as we celebrated his 60th birthday on the 5th of February 2011 life was about to change forever.

Mum went to the toilet and collapsed in the hallway and the dance of life as we knew it ended. She had a massive stroke, emergency surgery overnight and 2 weeks in Intensive Care at the Alfred Hospital. Her quality of life was gone with little movement and no signs of communication. During these two weeks I held her hand, talked to her and said "choose what's best for you, Mum". We as a family knew she would not want to live as a vegetable and made the decision to turn off the life support and let her choose her own journey. She died 4 hours later.

Nothing could prepare me for the grief that followed. "Mum Moments" are part of my journey as I discover my way to keep in touch with her as I continue my life.

- - - - - - -

As the days unfolded with Mum in Intensive Care I found a beautiful French notebook and jotted notes as my thoughts flowed.

This notebook, along with any paper or pen close by, became the inspiration for my "Mum Moments".

"Mum Moments" became my salvation whether it was a thought, an object or a feeling that brought me into my Mum Moments' space.

- - - - - - -

MUM MOMENTS – FEELINGS & THOUGHTS

Monday 7th February 2011 - morning

I walked into my room this morning to find something she has given me to hold on to and realised there was no need to hold on. "I am surrounded by her love". She is everywhere. She touches everyone.

Progress is slow and the next 24 hours will give the answers.

I know in my heart it is time to let her go and let her make the next choice on her journey.

I am in and out of grief, sobbing at times, feeling her and knowing that in Spirit she is exactly where she needs to be right now.

I want my Mummy back and I know it's time to let her go and make her own choices.

- - - - - - -

Fawkner Park – Monday 7th February 2011 - 1:20 pm

I honour all the names you choose

Mum

Shirley Barbara Martin

Michaela

I love you Mum

- - - - - - -

Michaela

I am surrounded by your love.

Bless you,

Love Jude

I am having a picnic with my Mum.

- - - - - - -

In My Garden – *Thursday 10th February 2011 - 11:10 am*

Mum choose whatever is best for you…………

I am with you always.

Love Jude

- - - - - - -

I am having a cup of tea and toast with My Mum listening to Secret Garden.

- - - - - - -

Wednesday 16th February 2011

May the sun shine brightly in your heart as you continue on your journey.

Love Jude

- - - - - - -

5 Beautiful Daughters

5 Unique Personalities

Let them all Shine

In their own way.

Love you Mum

Jude

- - - - - - -

Sunday 20th February 2011 - 1:28 pm

I Bless you and release you on your Journey Mum.

- - - - - - -

Thursday 24th February 2011

In early 2011, as I was cleaning up, I found a note I had written to my mother in 2006.

- - - - - - -

On the day of her funeral I chose to share the letter as we celebrated her life:

Dear Mum,

Thank you for my life, for all that you are and all that you can be.

Your love and kindness and generosity have seen me ride many a wave in my life.

Your love and compassion has helped me to understand the importance of life and all that there is to be gracious for.

My love for you is unconditional and will see me through all that life presents for me.

I treasure each and every experience we have had together. I value the highs and lows and valuable lessons on this life's journey.

My grace and your grace will carry us through as the adventure continues.

With Love,

Jude

- - - - - - -

Friday 25th February 2011

The day after Mum's funeral on the 24th February 2011 I went into my denial phase of unbelievable heartache and pain that she was no longer going to walk up my driveway ever again. It was a deep dark hole in my memory broken on the 11th March 2011 when I was going about my business and I got a firm voice in my head saying "Cross the Road".

My response was "I don't want to but okay I will."

I crossed the road and walked into a healing centre and a beautiful woman took me under her wings and helped me to open up to the power of healing through spiritual connection.

I thank my Mum for saying "Cross the Road Jude"

- - - - - - -

Saturday 26th March 2011

'Let us dance in the sun, wearing wild flowers in our hair.'

Marcello and Monique

Bloomsville

'You will always be a beautiful flower in the posy I hold in my hand.'

Marcello X

- - - - - - -

Bloomsville

A wonderful flower and gift shop had become a special place for Mum in recent years and I thank Marcello and Monique for their love and creativity.

In the early days after Mum's death I found solace and connection walking into this beautiful space. My notebook came from Bloomsville and I was deeply touched by the words they wrote in it. These words resonated with the woman I loved.

Connected

In Tune

Peaceful

Spending some time with Mum.

Blackburn Lake

- - - - - - -

Sunday 27th March 2011

Music

I love you Mum and I feel loved by you.

- - - - - - -

Mum Moments

Out of Africa Music

"Let the rest of the world go by"

Your photo – I am surrounded by your love.

- - - - - - -

I feel you, I hear you, I see you.

I Love You

Enjoy your day

Love Jude

- - - - - - -

Wednesday 30th March 2011

Bath – Nurturing

Candle

Mum Mantra

Love

Home

- - - - - - -

"Mum Moments" April 2011

Thursday 14th April 2011 - 2:55 pm

This journal is a dedication and celebration of the life I shared with:

Shirley Barbara Cain (birth name)

Shirley Barbara Martin (married name)

Mum

Gran

Michaela (her chosen spiritual name)

On earth as we know it and an opportunity to share "Mum Moments" as we journey a new pathway together.

- - - - - - -

Fond Memories are alive and well.

Shining Through

Healing with a friend

I Love You Mum

Judy

- - - - - -

Angel Heart ...

Clarissa ...

Women Who Run With the Wolves ...

I Love You Mum

Jude

- - - - - - -

I love you Mum

- - - - - - -

Saturday 16th April 2011 - 2:55 pm

Mum died 8 weeks ago and I am having a Mum Moment right now.

There have been many "Mum Moments" over the last ten weeks since she had a massive stroke.

Moments before we were dancing on the dance floor to my husband's band as he celebrated his 60th birthday.

We were shining together as we celebrated and enjoyed the freedom of dance.

I can see her now. I can feel her now. I am surrounded by her love as I miss her physical presence in my life.

I am learning to communicate with her on a soul level, embracing the spiritual essence of life that we so often discussed.

Intuitively I know she is here guiding me when I stop to listen and in the background waiting for me to be ready to be guided by her wisdom.

How blessed I am that she introduced me to the power of love, the power of touch and the stillness to be found within us all.

As I write, the sun shines through the clouds and the signs she taught me to appreciate the simple things in life are alive and well everywhere.

Judy Taylor

- - - - - - -

Sunday 17th April 2011

Mum you always believed in me, even when I didn't believe in myself. Thank you.

Jude

- - - - - - -

Saturday 23rd April 2011

Driving with Mum

Enjoying her love of Eltham.

Special Places

Shillinglaw Cottage

Birds, Peace, Tranquility.

Beauty within and without.

The Light Factory Gallery and Tea House

Shine a Light on Me

Montsalvat

Spooky, calm, surreal

Deep, cultural, ancestral

Open Book

Peaceful - Serene

Mia Mia Aboriginal Art Gallery and Café

Speed Humps ☺

The Freedom to roam

The Spirit

Women's Meeting Place

Quiet time with my Mum

Thank you

Jude

- - - - - - -

Easter Sunday - 24th April 2011 - Jan Juc

Writing in the sand.

Walking alone on the beach.

Café Latte's

Sunshine

Stars

Ocean

Laughter

Cruising, peace and tranquility

- - - - - - -

Saturday 30th April 2011

I danced all night with Mum at Elwood RSL last night.

I could feel her everywhere. Her presence was calming, loving and moving.

Moments of tears flowed with moments of joy as we journeyed a new life together.

- - - - - - -

Sunday 1st May 2011

Relaxing in bed.

Enjoying a bath.

Together in Love.

I am surrounded by her love.

- - - - - - -

Monday 2nd May 2011

Hi Mum,

Today I instinctively went to call you and realised I couldn't.

I went for a walk with Tye and you were right there with me.

Walking back I felt so good and a beautiful purple flower presented.

I am feeling so happy.

It's wonderful having a soul relationship with you.

Love Jude

- - - - - - -

Saturday 7th May 2011

Dear Mum,

Yesterday I bought a laptop computer especially for me.

I am so excited that I have found another way to communicate with you.

I Love You

Jude

- - - - - - -

Yum ... Café latte and flourless orange cake with Mum at Caffe Romeo

- - - - - - -

Tuesday 17th May 2011

Pure Bread Bakery – John and Me

A Mum Moment

Latte and flourless orange cake

- - - - - - -

Monday 23rd May 2011

Today I had a milestone moment with my daughter – just the sort of moment I would love to share with my Mum.

Shared it with husband ... nice, however would love to share that special experience with my Mum.

- - - - - - -

Friday 27th May 2011

Do you know my Mum?

To me she was Mum.

Others knew her as Gran, Shirley and Michaela.

A wonderful woman who chose to leave this earth and life as we know it three months ago.

I haven't read a book since then. I lie in bed most nights with her in my thoughts.

Sometimes I can feel her and sometimes I cannot.

My mind is so busy with thoughts of things to do that I stop myself from being still and sharing with her.

Sharing our new journey at times feels quite normal and at other times so distant that I just want to reach out and touch her.

Sometimes I just want my Mummy back. Sometimes I just ache to see her, feel her, cuddle her, touch her and be with her.

The tears flow freely as I allow myself to be with her and be with my thoughts.

I am sitting in a cafe that I know she would love if she was here with me and I know in many ways she guided me here today.

We are so in tune. I know her, she knows me, we know each other and this intuitive knowing is still here and will continue forever.

In the stillness she will always be here for me and even when I am busy, she is here waiting for me, waiting to share, waiting to love, and waiting to give me wisdom to guide me as I continue to live my life.

Bless you Mum. I love you so much. I miss you being here physically and I thank you for sharing your experience of spirituality so I can continue to share with you on a soul level.

I love you Mum.

Jude

- - - - - - -

Sunday 29th May 2011

Mum and I shared the Tibetan Monk Chant experience this morning at Box Hill and the wonder of the creation of the Mandala.

A book "Advice on Dying and Living a Better Life" by His Holiness the Dalai Lama presented to me and I knew it was for me right now.

When I asked the price my resistance was strong and my money issues got in the way as I chose to walk away.

Before far my inner knowing encouraged me to overcome, step outside my money issues and return to buy the book.

This book is a gift of peace for me, a gift from my Mum, a gift from the Dalai Lama, a gift from the Universe.

Again I am being reminded I am being guided by the Power of Love every day.

Be still and Listen.

Thank you Mum

- - - - - - -

Wednesday 1st June 2011 - Montsalvat

As I sit and contemplate the beautiful day at Montsalvat, I relish in the sunshine and the beauty before me.

I am reminded of the times you visited and the love you experienced as you sat in the silence and contemplated the day.

Lyrebirds are present and in the moment add colour serenity and beauty to the surroundings.

Children explore and discover the magic in every moment. Others sit and share in the garden cafe as time passes by and the natural sounds of nature permeate the day.

- - - - - - -

Thursday 9th June 2011

Relaxing in the bath on my son's Birthday and thinking of Dad lying in hospital. I had a really strong feeling to go to Marcello's and Mum would guide me to a gift for Dad. A gift from me and a gift from Mum.

A phone call to Marcello and he was not going to be there. Life unfolded and I did not make it there.

This morning I was reminded to take a gift from me and Mum so headed to Bloomsville to see Marcello. Divine timing, he was there and a Mum style ... Jude style gift presented.

Marcello and I shared a coffee and beautiful moment just as Mum and he had done on many occasions.

Then my journey continues to the hospital. The giraffe has Mum's energy and I can feel her everywhere. The little rattle in his neck helps me tune into her.

Life is good.

- - - - - - -

Wednesday 29th June 2011

I am very raw. I think I am trying to hide my pain rather than feel it. A good friend rang me this morning and I was explaining how I was feeling when we got cut off. I have been feeling raw ever since.

Her call was not by chance. It was an opportunity to open up and feel, to go with my intuition and start listening again to my guides, my angels, and my mum who are trying to help me through this astronomical change in my life. They are trying to give me the assistance to get through this loss, this pain, this sadness I am feeling at the loss of my mother. This woman who loved me no matter what, who supported me through the highs, lows, in betweens and the downright horrible at times. This woman who knew me, all of me and loved every single part of me. I need her, I want her, I love her and miss her. The pain is so raw. It is indescribable.

- - - - - - -

Friday 1st July 2011

What a beautiful woman you are, so loved, so precious, so gorgeous.

I am blessed to have you as my Mum.

Forever with Me

Forever In My heart

Forever and Ever

Love Jude

- - - - - - -

Eltham Cemetery

By the Pond

Our Special Place

Time Together

Time to Share

Time to Love

Thursday 14th July 2011

I'm sitting in the Sandbar Café in Middle Park with windows to the right and windows to the left that open up to the ocean on one side and the world on the other. What an amazing feeling to be sitting here writing on my computer. The feeling of freedom is incredible as I allow myself to write as I type. A foreign step for me in many ways as traditionally writing has come for me from pen, paper and my hands as I allow my thoughts to flow. There is definitely a difference ... viva la difference. I am discovering that it is possible for me to write and type as well as being aware of my surroundings and the sun shining and the background conversation as everyone here experiences their own day.

Sitting observing some elderly ladies sipping on their coffee as they chat. This is what mum loved to do with her friends and she would be in her element here with the warmth of the sun on the window and the ocean as a backdrop. I reflect, I am right in my element here too. I know how she would feel because I am connected to her on an energetic level ... always have been and always will be.

Acceptance of her physical passing is a necessity for me to embrace as time goes by in order for me to connect with her on a daily basis. It is amazing. It is like she is talking to me, sending these messages to me as I allow myself to write. The freedom, the connection is boundless and I see how the flatness and vulnerability that was presenting to me as we drove here dissipates as soon as I tune into what is around me. My fingers are flowing on the typewriter as quickly as they have learnt to write over the last 56 years. Listening, feeling and writing come naturally to me when I just do it without thought.

- - - - - - -

The John Denver Story

Friday 15th July 2011

Best Seats in the house, front row of the Balcony was the only place for me to experience the John Denver Story. To feel his magic, to feel his connection, to relate to his life as Rick Price shared John's life and the music he sang to express himself throughout his life.

I have loved John Denver's songs throughout my life. His songs resonate with me and my own life experiences.

Joy, laughter and tears flowed as I sang his songs, listened to his stories and felt mum's presence as the show played on.

A gamut of emotions ... all of them flowed freely just like John Denver's songs. Lifting the spirit, soaring to places I have never been. Knowing those places - a higher ground he called it - exist for one and all when we allow our spirits to soar.

His time on this earth ended before we were ready. However, in perfect harmony, it was time for him to move on.

Mum too ... her journey here was to close like the chapter in a good book leaving us wanting for more. Her new chapter, her new journey has begun and when I am ready to journey with her the new story will begin. It has already begun. Like a good book sitting by your bedside waiting for you to open it, Mum is waiting everyday for me to open the book on our new journey.

Knowing how beautifully she wrote and how I write we have a strong connection to communicate with each other. In any moment she can speak to me and through me as I open to channeling her.

I do not know where this is going and how it will unfold but I owe it to myself and to the glory of my Mum to spread my wings and fly.

- - - - - - -

Wednesday 20th July 2011

As I journey through my life, one common theme keeps presenting: people saying "you should write". Okay let's take the should out of it. I am writing now and it's great. Have a wonderful day.

- - - - - - -

Monday 25th July 2011

In My Head In The Middle Of The Night

What

When

Where

In my stillness I create

In the Moment

Reach out and touch somebody's hand, make this world a better place if you can ...   *(memory of a Diana Ross song)*

Create a space and they will come

Tye (our dog) always believes

Through vulnerability comes Inner Strength

Intuitive Moments

Gratitude

Celestine Prophecy

I am the change I need

Write Write Write

I Love it

Doing what I love to do

Not just for me

Living in the Moment

Advice on Dying

Living ... Dying ... Impermanence ...

Daily Diary

Judy's Diary

Space ☺

Living and Dying

The journey between

My mission is to write

What?

Write ☺

Change your perspective and you can change the colour of your day ☺

Intuitive Knowing

Thank you

"Mum Moments" – Me Moments

A time to explore

A time to be still

A time to love

- - - - - - -

Friday 29th July 2011

Holistic Healing has been an important part of my life for many years. However nothing could prepare me for this journey since my mother's sudden death in February 2011.

The joy of dancing with her on the dance floor changed dramatically when she collapsed in the hallway of the Elwood RSL, an ambulance was called and she was rushed to the Alfred Hospital. Emergency Surgery we were told was the only option with no guarantees. A massive stroke had occurred with a bleed on the brain. The best outcome we could hope for would unfold over the next 24 to 48 hours. This did not present a positive future. Over the next 2 weeks every family member had the opportunity to spend time with her in ICU and experience their own journey and grief as it became clear that her physical and cognitive recovery was not to be.

I often sat with her in these times loving her, cuddling her stroking her and saying "I love you Mum, choose what's best for you."

As a family we chose to turn off her life support and let her make the choice. She died 4 hours later.

We celebrated her life with a wonderful ceremony at Wattle Park with well over 200 people from all walks of life who had walked her journey.

The day after her funeral I was hit by complete and total denial. I could not believe she was not going to walk up the driveway. I could not feel her spirit. I could not feel her soul. I just wanted my mum. I ached for my mum. I cried for my mum I wanted my mum. I could not connect with her I could not hear her. I just ached.

- - - - - - -

Sunday 7th August 2011

Mum Moments – Creatures of Habit

Conservatory Cafe – Botanical Gardens

I chose a corner table by the window in the café and discovered the table no was 7. My lucky number. I like corner tables and often gravitate to them.

I ordered a strong latte and flourless orange cake to touch my taste buds. As usual I needed some extra hot milk in the jug to temper the strong flavour. I enjoyed every sip and every bite as I read some articles in a magazine that interested me.

Observing my surroundings and the people around me, my thoughts flowed with my own life experiences and feelings.

A young boy sitting with his parents all in their own world and their own experiences. Watching him sip on his chocolate milk drink brought a smile to my face as he tasted it and played with it. A young girl contemplating a heavy door and a smile from an elderly lady. A middle aged man and woman helping a much older man to his feet after enjoying their muffin and coffee. Some war veterans (that's what they looked like to me) sharing lunch with their wives and I'm sure some stories to tell.

Grandmothers, mothers, daughters and sons sharing a moment. Table talk ... I like it.

A helping hand for a lady carrying a tray opening the sliding door for her with a friendly exchange. Human interaction can be such a pleasure.

As I look around laughter and smiles abound. Thought provoking conversations to be had amongst quiet contemplation at other tables.

The sun finds a way to shine through a cloudy day and the world is at peace for me right now.

Living in the present moment with quiet contemplation can bring joy to the heart and a smile to the face. What a wonderful way to spend my day.

Nature calls and its time to move on.

- - - - - - -

Sunday 7th August 2011

Let My Spirit Sing

I am with you always

You are surrounded by my love

No one can take that away from you

From the moment we connected

Our spirits were entwined forever and beyond

Our journey has changed

But we are together everyday

Feel me as you live your life

Know I am right beside you every step of the way

Take a moment to be still and you can feel my presence

Feel my Love

Feel our Connection

Love will conquer all

Shining in my own way

Treasure the words "I love you"

I can hear you say my name

See my smiling face

Dance with me

Close your eyes and remember the times I brought a smile to your face

Remember I am always with you

Our journey has changed

My spirit lives with you everyday

Remember I am always with you

In your quiet moments

You can hear me

You can talk to me

Remember where we have been

Know we are together

As we discover our new way.

- - - - - - -

Tuesday 9th August 2011

I can't believe this pain. It takes me completely by surprise. I don't know where it's coming from and then I'm sobbing uncontrollably. I miss my Mum so much. How can someone so alive be so dead? I didn't realise just how deep this pain is and how it continues to manifest in my body.

I'm sitting in bed writing this with my Mum's shawl. Well, it's mine really. She gave it to me as a gift sometime ago and I've slept with it, cuddling it every night since she had her stroke and died.

Dead, it's just so hard to believe she's gone. I can feel her here, there and everywhere.

I'm surrounded by her love, surrounded by her, her touch, her smell, her kindness, her smile, her everything.

Dead is such a funny word really. What does it really mean? She's dead but she feels so alive to me, so present, so personable, so amazing and so dead. It doesn't really make any sense to me. She's so beautiful, so loving, so caring, so loved, so lovable, so annoying, so there and yet so gone. Gone where, gone why, gone somewhere, gone beyond here, gone beyond our knowing, gone to a better place, gone from here forever.

Gone, gone, gone and I don't want her gone. I want her here, I want her now. I want her forever and ever and ever.

I don't care about impermanence. I don't care that life doesn't last forever. I want her to last forever and ever.

She's my Mum and I want her here, I want her now and I want her forever and ever and ever. I feel like a two year old who wants her lollies and I do want my lollies and I want my Mummy and I want her now.

She's my Mum. I love her and I want her now, right now.

- - - - - - -

Friday 12th August 2011

Grief Research

Birth and Death are part of life and since my mother died six months ago I have discovered that grief is too.

You can read about them all however nothing can prepare you for how you experience these events when they actually happen.

Grief has taken me by surprise, and as I experience all that it is for me I am writing my story and recognising it is a powerful tool in the healing process.

Saturday 13th August 2011

Lilies On Brougham - Eltham

"Your Mum was beautiful, we loved her.

My Mum died 8 years ago and it's like 8 minutes ago."

(Lady at Lilies ...)

Thought for my book – "Living and Grieving"

Saturday 27th August 2011

Mum, what were you doing ... what were you feeling 56 years ago ... the day before I was born?

- - - - - - -

Wednesday 7th September 2011 - 3:30 pm

The white dove that hangs on my bedroom window was a gift from you.

The tulip that is about to open in the pot on the front porch ... another gift from you.

I am surrounded by reminders of your magic touch and the physical presence of the gifts you generously chose for me.

I can feel the warmth of the spring sunshine on my back as I sit in the front yard thinking of you. Your warmth of character and the joy you brought to me and others in your time on earth will carry me and everyone as we continue our lives.

Our journey has changed ... the magic of you will live forever.

Bless you Mum. I love you.

Jude

Friday 23rd September 2011

As I walk through the park and sit in the garden I am reminded of you.

Spring is in the air and the yellow daisies covering the ovals remind me of the daisy chains we made when I was a child. The pretty little flowers that cover the lawns ... I call them wild flowers and they remind me of you.

I remember going to the tulip festival last year with you. I remember the joy you experienced in the garden and the pleasure you experienced from buying flowers for your home and others.

The tulips you gave me for my birthday last year presented as a bud just before my birthday.

One beautiful tulip in full bloom has given me the gift of joy from you.

You gave so much joy to others in your lifetime and in the sadness of your loss we remember your joy

Love Jude

- - - - - - -

Saturday 24th September 2011

I wish I'd gone with you in the ambulance.

Never in my wildest dreams did I expect you would die.

I still can't believe it.

I don't want to believe it.

I want you here.

I want you now.

I miss you so much.

I'm so boring.

I'm so alone without you.

I love you Mum.

Please come back to me.

The pain is unbearable.

- - - - - - -

7 months

7 minutes

7 is my lucky number

7 ways to say I love you

7 ways whatever

Mum Moments

There are many

Some happy

Some sad

Some take you completely by surprise

Some don't

- - - - - - -

Sunday 6th November 2011

Sitting in Cavallini Cafe at the round table in the window contemplating as I wait for a latte and almond croissant. I love this place. You introduced me to it more than 12 months ago and the flavour of Cavallini has stayed with me ever since.

It is the little things that touch us and stay with us forever.

You touched me Mum ... so many times in our lifetime and you will stay with me forever.

Love Jude

- - - - - - -

Early January 2012

"Life is what happens while you are busy making other plans"

2010 ended with a great night at the Mitcham RSL for me, our daughter and John whilst our son enjoyed doing his own thing. John's band played great music as we all danced the night away.

My Mum and Dad came along for an hour and ended up staying all night, which is a testament to the band's great music along with the good company. Mum enjoyed hitting the dance floor with me and other friends and Dad said he was looking forward to joining us for a dance when his new prosthetic leg had settled in.

It was a wonderful start to 2011.

In January 2011 we had a great holiday at Tootgarook followed by many hours watching the Australian Tennis Open and generally enjoying the summer holidays.

John turned 60 in January and decided it would be fun to celebrate his birthday at the band's next gig at Elwood RSL on the 5th February. Friends from Melbourne and interstate, together with many members of my family, came along to enjoy the evening. What a night it was – good food, good wine, good company and lots of dancing. We were also looking forward to carrying on into the night as we hadn't seen many of these people in too long a time.

And then the unthinkable happened. Just before midnight I was dancing with Mum on the dance floor, the band went to a break and Mum headed to the toilet. Unfortunately she never made it as she collapsed in the hallway. That was the beginning of a rollercoaster for me that is almost indescribable as Mum had a massive stroke. The next two weeks were spent in ICU at the Alfred Hospital and we soon came to the realisation that it was time to let her go. She died on the 20th February 2011.

―――

This has had such a phenomenal affect on my life. Mum and I had lived every emotion under the sun during our time together; some good, some not so good, and through it all we had developed a wonderful sharing relationship. Our deep commitment to spirituality had a profound effect on both our lives and her journey as Shirley Barbara Martin, Mum, Gran - and her chosen spiritual name Michaela - enriched so many people who valued her contribution to their life.

On a physical level I have experienced so much pain at her loss. On a spiritual level I know she is always with me. My love of writing has supported me as I express my feelings through my "Mum Moments" Journal. It has been my guiding light through the highs and lows of grief.

Mum died doing what she loved ... dancing ... and I celebrate that in my best moments. In my worst moments I say: "how can someone so alive be so dead?" At these times I long for her presence here with me right now. I look forward to the moments when I appreciate fully that she is always here with me.

And that is how 2011 unfolded.

So many positives have presented in 2011:

We are healthy.

We have regular income.

I am writing, recently returned to regular meditation, walking regularly by myself or with our gorgeous dog, Tye.

- - - - - - -

Moving On

Day to day life with my family has seen us all grow and develop in our own personal ways.

Renovations to our house have started this week and we are looking forward to the extra space. Having two adults and two teenagers sharing one entertainment area presents challenges so our renovated studio will give us two comfortable spaces to enjoy. Last year we contemplated selling up & moving on, but we all agreed that we love it here and that we live in the best possible position for our family right now.

May your Christmas, New Year and the coming year be filled with joy, happiness and laughter.

John often comments on John Lennon's saying: "Life is what happens while you are busy making other plans" As 2011 comes to a close I can definitely say "I can relate to that"

- - - - - - -

Saturday 14th January 2012

"Let me go Jude…………………"

Just before midnight on the 13th of January 2012 in tones so sweet my Mum said those words to me. I had just finished reading a great novel and laying it down beside my bed to go to sleep.

Her voice was so clear, the way she says Jude resonates with me and I know it's her. She is connecting with me in a way she knows I will hear her and know it is her.

So many times over the past twelve months I've wanted to feel her, touch her, have her and longed for our new way of life to not be real.

I've wanted to experience what others have shared with me. Many people experience a loved one that has died as a human figure sitting beside them in the garden, the lounge room, on the edge of their bed guiding them, helping them, loving them.

It's not like that for me.

She's everywhere for me but not in the physical human form. I can feel her everywhere, it's a knowing of her presence, her love, her support, her spirit is alive and well. The physical is gone and replaced with a part of her that will never leave me, never abandon me and will live forever.

I am blessed she gave me this gift to live with her presence for the rest of my life.

- - - - - - -

Sunday 29th January 2012

Hey Mum, you'd laugh at me I can see your smile. I was enjoying a frolic on this hot summer's day in the waterfall by your grave.

It's the sort of thing I can imagine you doing, dipping your painted toenails in the cool fresh water, enjoying the sound of the birds, watching the butterflies, loving the beauty you are surrounded by.

Peace and serenity in the moment – the ultimate experience.

I love the feeling of peace and serenity and it feels so good when I give myself the time to be in the moment.

Thank you for introducing me to the wonders of life.

I'm sitting at Lilies with an icepack on my leg about to order a latte. In the frivolity of the moment I slipped and landed on a rock. I'm laughing at myself because I wouldn't have missed the moment whatever the consequence.

I love you Mum.

Jude

- - - - - - -

I'm sitting observing the surroundings at Lilies and watching people enjoying the moment. A lady that reminds me of you ... two little girls enjoying lunch with their Mum ... and the background chatter of others... such a lovely place to be.

- - - - - - -

Sunday 5th February 2012

Twelve months ago my life was about to turn upside down ... upside down forever ... The life I knew with you was gone.

As I come full circle 12 months on I realise the physical loss is as raw today as it was then.

Sitting in Cavallini Café your presence is strong. I am surrounded by you in all that I see and all that I feel. The people, the music, the food, the sounds, the warm windy weather ... they all remind me of you.

A mother who gave so much, shared so much, touched me so much that you will stay with me forever.

Love Jude

- - - - - - -

I would like to celebrate the life of a woman who is described by many as "the most wonderful woman I have ever met in my life"

Her capacity to love and be loved touched the heart and soul of everyone who met her.

To me she was Mum, others new her as Gran, Shirley and Michaela.

- - - - - - -

Tuesday 14th February 2012 - 11:59 am

As the day unfolds and my awareness of where I was 12 months ago living with the shock of Mum's stroke and pending death, my intuition said go to Jan Juc – you need some time for you.

So I did it. I sent the sms:

"Hi M, hope u r well. I was wondering if Jan Juc is available sat/sun night. Mum died 12 mths ago next Monday and I need some time alone. Judy"

- - - - - - -

Wednesday 15th February 2012 - 6:00 pm

Hi Jude Jan Juc is available call me re key as I need 2 organise it by 2morr NA Fri thanx M

- - - - - -

Wednesday 15th February 2012 - 8:43 pm

Hi M, feeling vulnerable 2day re weekend by myself & my mum thoughts. Have lm 4 my friend 2 see if she is free 2 come with me. Will call u 2morro after sleeping on it.

Part of me thinks good 2 go alone & part feels vulnerable. Jude xoxo

- - - - - - -

My vulnerability was alive and well. My resistance even greater. I was being challenged at the highest level to plunge into me.

The universe provided my friend was unavailable.

My need to listen to my intuition was as strong as ever. I got to "Go for It" and I did I made the phone call and the best weekend I could possibly have presented itself.

- - - - - - -

Friday 17th February 2012 - 10:20 am

Going away with Mum for the weekend. Really looking forward to spending time with you.

Thank you for introducing me to Energy work.

I have just spent some time with my good friend and acknowledged I connect with Mum through voice messages.

I am so happy I am writing my journal.

- - - - - - -

Saturday 18th February 2012

Daytime – Mum Moments

Coffee

Waiting

Sharing

Tasting

Cycling

Singing

Walking

Beach

Paddling

Walking

Loving

Singing

Bike riding

Wedding - Mum moments sharing with a lady minding her grandchild while her daughter was a bridesmaid.

Sharing my Mum – she shared her pain at loss of child – cot death - over 20 years ago – Compassion was flowing.

Sunset

- - - - - - -

Saturday 18th February 2012 - 5:55 pm

Walking, Talking, Feeling,

I never knew how good it could be.

Walking, Singing, Feeling,

I know how good it can be.

Dancing, laughing, crying,

I never knew how much they feel.

Feeling, Feeling, Feeling,

I feel you everywhere

Your beautiful voice resonates in all that I do

I can feel, I can love you every single day.

In the silence of the night, I will reflect on my day ...

- - - - - - -

Sunday 19th February 2012 - Around 10:00 am

Relaxing on front porch

Drew an Angel card – "Answered Prayer"

Precious Earth Journal – a gift from Mum – opened it ...

"The wind that gave our grandfather his first breath also receives his last sight" *(from Chief Seattle's Famous Speech)*

Chamomile Tea

Beetle wanders across page ... amazing

I-pod shuffle

Tango to Evora – Loreena McKennitt

You're nobody till somebody loves you – Michael Buble

Lionel Ritchie – Outrageous ... "laughs the ways she works that body ... scandalous ..."

Keith Urban – Days go By ..."so you better start living right now ... we think about forever only got today..."

Amazing understanding, compassion and love

The peace and serenity of the surroundings is amazing as life happens around me. Sound of the birds, children at play, adults – some busy in their activities ... others relaxing ... all living in the moment.

- - - - - - -

12:05 pm

Sometimes the pain, that gut wrenching feeling in your solar plexus takes me completely by surprise.

Relaxing at Insalt Café in Torquay overlooking the ocean, latte in hand and it's there, that feeling of loss ... the sadness that has surprised me at any given moment since your death 12 months ago.

It's a reminder to value every given moment and embrace every feeling.

The waves come in and the waves go out. It's a natural process to experience our feelings.

With Love

Jude

Sunday 19th February 2012 - 12:20 pm

I love to share, I love to hear,

I love to be, I love people,

In the moment I am blessed.

I never want to go home ... oh that's scary! What does it mean? Home to the home that I've known? The home where no-one knows me? The home where no love exists? The home where I am alone?

My home is full of love, understanding and caring. My home is now in the moment. I am at home wherever I am.

- - - - - - -

12:40 pm

A play – In the Moment

Mum Moments

One person main character – Many faces of a wonderful woman

- - - - - - -

"I'm just like her"

- Cute
- Dancing
- Shopping – friends of Michaela
- Family – Shirley
- The Gatherer
- Nurturing

I have all of her wonderful characteristics and all of her annoying ones depending on your perspective.

12:50 pm

Home – home is a place in your heart ☺

2:47 pm

Yesterday is a dream tomorrow is a vision. Today is the moment.

Judy with Michaela

Sunday 19th February 2012 - 2:50 pm

Write it as it is and see what unfolds

Judy with Michaela

- - - - - - -

2:52 pm

You will know when to write them. Go and have some fun.

With Love Judy and Michaela

- - - - - - -

2:59 pm

Me and Mum, walking on the beach, singing Diana Ross and John Denver songs

- - - - - - -

4:43 pm

Channeling Michaela through Jude with John

- - - - - - -

5:23 pm

Michaela with Jude – "there's nothing to fix"

- - - - - - -

Sharing conversation with travellers

Vietnam – Dalat – Paradise Lake – Buddhist Temple – lake, mountains

She knew about Community Human Spirit

If it feels good – Intuition is saying "do it"

- - - - - - -

Monday 20th February 2012 - 8:00 am

I've lit my candle

I've played our songs

I've cried our tears

I've had our cup of tea

I'm sitting on the balcony

I'm surrounded by the sounds of nature

And most of all I'm missing you

There, it's out. Once I've acknowledged it, once I've felt it, once I've said it ... "I'm missing you Mum" ... a peace and serenity has replaced the pain.

Over the past few days at Jan Juc and Torquay I have come up close and personal with you. Singing songs, walking along the beach, sipping on lattes, relaxing. Sharing your magic wherever I go.

There have been high times and low times, laughter and tears. I have encompassed all that I am and all I can be.

Between you and me we have known every emotion as we've journeyed on earth. Death, like living, has given me the chance to be up close and personal with who I am.

Thank you for giving birth to me. Thank you for loving me. Thank you for knowing me. Thank you for understanding me. Thank you for being my Mum.

I love you so much.

Jude

- - - - - - -

Saturday 25th February 2012 - around midday

In the post office 3 elderly ladies who seem so old – it takes me completely by surprise the feelings that erupt in me. It takes my breath away. Why are they here and you gone? It takes my breath away. You were so young compared to them. Yet they are here and you are gone.

Over the past twelve months it's the little things that trigger emotions and challenge me to get in touch with what is real for me, to dig deep and find my inner truth, to believe what I believe and follow my heart home.

- - - - - - -

Tuesday 28th February 2012

It's my time right now to take all my hand written writing and type it out so I can share it with the world.

As I type, my words are unfolding and resonating with me and I feel the person within me and the beauty of who I am. It's astounding how wonderful I feel. I am me and I am love.

My "Mum Moments" are so beautiful. They bring tears to my eyes and take my breath away.

- - - - - - -

Thursday 8th March 2012 - 9:55 am

You're here everywhere, I can feel you, I can see you, I can love you.

Clearing out my healing room for our renovations.

As we open up our lives and create a space for a more peaceful and comfortable living environment for us all, I can see you smiling down on us.

Our dreams and visions that we have held onto for so long are manifesting and enriching our lives.

So many lovely pieces you have given me. So many books you have given me and some you have lent me – all I will care for and treasure for the rest of my life.

I love you Mum

- - - - - - -

Sunday 11th March 2012 - 10:50 am

My body is aching. My resistance to get back to compiling my "Mum Moments" is strong. My excuses are many.

The pain is as deep as I know when a simple conversation yesterday turns to tears when I say: "I was dancing on the dance floor with my Mum just over 12 months ago before she had a massive stroke".

The tears are raw and oh so powerful, they grab me and there's no escape.

Everything is challenging me right now; the good things and the bad things all are presenting challenges in my life.

It all feels so overwhelming but most of all I'm overwhelmed by my loss of you.

I miss you Mum – no one can take that away from me.

I Love you Mum.

Jude

- - - - - - -

Sitting on my balcony with a cup of Chamomile tea as a white butterfly flies by. You're with me Mum ... I know it, but the pain is still here.

- - - - - - -

Saturday 17th March 2012

Diamonds have flaws and that makes them unique ☺

- - - - - - -

Sunday 1st April 2012

"Mum Moments" come and go. There is no rhyme or reason. Sometimes the moments are thoughts or feelings that I will hold in my heart forever. Other times the need to express through writing is alive and well. When pen and paper present the thoughts and feelings flow.

Writing is a wonderful way to connect with yourself and connect with a loved one who has died.

The power of love, the power of thought, the power of communicating with loved ones is amazing and truly significant for me as I journey life since my mother's death.

My writing has allowed me to experience grief and all that presents as I continue my life.

Exploring the emotions that present in my "Mum Moments" journal has and continues to heal me on a daily basis.

Sharing my journey thus far with you is important to me and I hope it will help you as you explore grief and the emotions it presents in your life.

- - - - - - -

Writing has been my most powerful healing tool as I journey my life without her and discover the magic of communicating with her even after death.

I still long for her kisses and cuddles, to see her smile or just say hello. However, that is not to be.

Yet when I am willing to stop and be with my "Mum Moments" her voice resonates in me and I'm reminded she's still here with me.

I still grieve, yet I am consoled by her presence and her love surrounds me.

I still weep and I still love … it's just different.

Sunday 29th April 2012

You are in my thoughts daily and I love it.

Often I need to write it, sometimes I do, sometimes I don't.

If it's meant to be I'll write it and if it's meant for me I'll keep it within me ... share it when it's right and keep it tight when it's not.

The wonder of writing is the fact that I can do it when the urge presents.

So often in life things come to me and I can see the benefit in sharing these thoughts. I understand the meaning, the truths that unfold in the moment.

I'm realising in the moment that sometimes the message is for me and sometimes the message is for sharing.

Intuitively I always know ... intuitively I sense that knowing.

I know it's time to listen more to me and allow my higher purpose on earth to be fulfilled.

Thank you for being my Mum.

Jude

Sunday 6th May 2012

"Write your journal ... "

The words resonate in my head as all the thoughts of the day present and I consider all the things I can do, should do, must do and need to do. Again clearly I get ... "write your journal"

How easy it is to ignore that voice ... the all-knowing inner voice that knows what's best for me.

I listened and here I am at Lilies with Mum, surrounded by her love, surrounded by her energy, surrounded by all the things that brought peace and serenity into her life.

I feel the same things. I sing the same songs. I am my mother's daughter and a wonderful woman ... just like she was.

I have my strengths and I have my weaknesses and that's what makes me whole.

- - - - - - -

"Why are you so busy trying to fit in when you were born to stand out?" *(from the movie 'What A Girl Wants')*

- - - - - - -

I spent time with my Mum today. She was present in my thoughts and present in the surroundings we shared.

As I was driving I pondered the thought ... "we had a love/hate relationship."

Hate - at times I intensely disliked her influence on my life.

Love – I immensely appreciate her influence on my life.

- - - - - - -

Monday 14th May 2012

Mother's Day – what a mish mash of feelings. My Mother's Day, your Mother's Day, everybody's Mothers' Day. What does it really mean?

As I ponder the day after, I recognise all it means. The highs, the lows, the happiness, the sadness, the memories of then, the memories of now.

Each experience we have as a mother moulds us as a person and helps us on the 'Mother Journey'. There are parts of the journey we love and parts we feel we could do without.

The parts we feel we could do without are probably our greatest gift as they encourage us to seek and find new directions for the greater benefit of all.

I missed you here with me yesterday ... your presence and your love was with me all day as always.

I love you Mum.

- - - - - -

Tuesday 15th May 2012

Dancing Ladies - beautiful flowers from Marcello at Bloomsville for Mother's Day.

I bought some of these beautiful flowers as a gift for myself and in memory of my gorgeous mum.

- - - - - - -

Wednesday 6th June 2012

I want my Mum

It's not fair

All these other people

Alive and kicking

And she's gone

It's not fair

I'm watching the Queen's Diamond Jubilee in London

And all these women

So much older than my Mum

They're alive and she's dead

It's not fair

I want my Mum

Why do all these people live so long

And my Mum's gone

It's not fair

I know it makes no sense

I know it's just the way it is

I want my Mum

It's not fair

I love you Mum

- - - - - -

Saturday 13th October 2012 - 12:10 pm

I have 'Mum Moments' everyday ... a piece of music, a vision of her that sometimes brings a smile and other times sadness. The wish that I could just give her a big cuddle and wanting her to be here.

I have been very caught up in the physical day to day world for several months and I need to connect with myself spiritually. I need to feel me, feel her in my life and get back to living in the moment.

- - - - - - -

Monday 15th October 2012 - 7:00 am

I feel teary and emotional

I just don't get it

Where do I find this joy I see in others

Where do I find this joy in me

I'm so sad

I'm so lonely

I'm so lost for me

Where do I find me

In this big wide world

Where oh where is me

Why do I feel so insignificant

So stuck in me with nowhere to go

Why do I feel not enough

Why do I feel so alone

Why oh why why me

Where do I go to find me

What do I do to find me

Why do I feel so alone

Oh me oh my why me

Where do I find the joy when I feel so alone

- - - - - -

Through pain and sorrow comes wisdom

The wisdom to see

The wisdom to know

The wisdom to love

The wisdom to give

The wisdom to be

The wisdom in me

- - - - - -

I see in you what I feel in me

- - - - - -

I feel so overwhelmed by all the day-to-days of life

Intuitively I get my next step

Physically I see all the things that need to be done

And my intuitive step pales into insignificance

It's like I'm wading through a jungle

I can see the light at the end

But the journey seems so overwhelming

That as I struggle through the twists and turns

And all the needs to be met along the way

The light at the end feels too far away

Exhausted I surrender

No, exhausted I give in

Exhausted I give in ... I give up.

And the light fades yet again

I sink into the swamp

I feel depleted

I've lost my way

I'm drowning in myself

While all the possibilities surround me

- - - - - -

Writing from within

Feeling the stuff that holds me

Feeling the stuff that blocks me

Feeling the stuff that is part of me

Feeling the stuff and moving on

Finding the joy that surrounds me

Finding the joy within me

Finding the joy that is me

- - - - - -

Monday 15th October 2012 - 7:32 am

Writing is my Joy

Love you Mum

Love Me

Love Life

- - - - - -

I love to write

It gives me a sense of me

It opens my heart

Opens my soul

Gives me a sense of who I am

Gives me a sense of who I am

Gives me a reason for living

Gives me a sense of knowing

Knowing this

Knowing that

Knowing all that I am

Knowing all that I can be

Knowing when

Knowing how

Knowing all that is me

Knowing I'm okay

Knowing I'm a shining light

Knowing I'm the way

Way to go

Way to be

Way to go to be me

Write it

Fight it

Light it

Block it

Open it

See it

Feel it

Be it

Be me

- - - - - -

A bundle of joy

A bundle of life

A bundle to unravel

- - - - - -

Hey Mum

Writing is my gift

A gift of love

A gift of life

A gift for everyone

Writing is my way

Writing is my me

Writing is my power

Writing is my strength

Writing is my way

Finding a way that resonates

Finding a way to be

Finding a way to be me

Finding a way to me

You know my life is like a landscape with undulating plains rolling over the oceans ...

- - - - - -

Wednesday 17th October 2012

I see a picture of you so clearly.

Everywhere I go you are there.

That beautiful physical picture of you.

I can't imagine that you are not here.

That you are gone for the rest of my life.

The physical you, the beautiful you, the wonderful you that I want to love, I want to touch, I want to cuddle and I can't.

The physical want is so strong right now that I find it hard to feel you physically and spiritually. The need for a way that cannot be is stopping me from being with you the way that it is.

It hurts, its painful. I'm blocking it because I want it the way it was and the way it was will never be the same again.

Help me Mum to find you, to feel you, to love you the way it is right now.

I'm grieving, I miss you Mum, I love you so much.

Love Jude

Saturday 20th October 2012

In the last week I have experienced every emotion under the sun and beyond.

The emotions perceived as negative in the world we live in have been the most positive in bringing me home to the joy in my heart.

Thank you to everyone who has been a part of my journey this week.

With love and appreciation.

Jude xoxoxo

- - - - - -

Sunday 21st October 2012

A good friend reminded me of the word 'gratitude' today. Let's share gratitude with all our friends and all their friends and send a wave of gratitude around the world.

- - - - - -

Sunday 28th October 2012 9:30 am

Writing for my life

I feel stuck – stuck in my own head with nowhere to go.

I feel inspirations and take them nowhere.

I feel inspired then I let it go.

Go where – I don't know.

Oh yes I do – there's a block in my head that rears its ugly head when I open my eyes to the possibilities.

As the inspiration flows, that voice in my head shuts it down with the day-to-day practicalities of getting through the day.

I feel stuck, stuck, stuck.

I should have been a builder as I've built so many walls in my life that I'm surrounded by 'stuck' in whatever direction I turn.

I see amazing things, I feel wonderful things. I have amazing things to share. I have wonderful things to share but I'm locked in, shut in, blocked by all the walls that stop me from living ... from being.

The walls rule me, they own me, they stuck me, they hurt me, they deflate me, they exhaust me, they stop me, they hurt me.

I'm stuck.

How do I unstuck me?

Bike ride

Walk

Journal – my journal ... write my journal.

- - - - - - -

Sunday 2nd December 2012

Life is wonderful. I just shared a fantastic walk with a good friend and my gorgeous dog Tye followed by a delicious latte. I love these experiences.

- - - - - -

Wednesday 26th December 2012 - Boxing Day

It's been a long journey since you passed away, since you moved on to a new life so far away. As I sit and ponder in my garden on a sunny Boxing Day, I can feel the warmth of the sunshine on my body. Tye sits faithfully by my side and a butterfly flies by.

Magnificent

Glorious

Divine

Beautiful

Loving

Gorgeous

And More

These are the things I experience in life.

I am blessed with the joy of knowing these feelings, feeling these feelings and being truly in touch with the wonder of life.

I enjoy these things every day of my life.

I have enjoyed all these things with you.

I have felt these feelings and I know you have too.

We are kindred spirits in life and in death.

Life and death bring feelings of joy and the depths of despair.

They are similar and different and all wound in one.

They are who we are and the feeling is the same.

A love of life is a wondrous feeling

A love of all creatures is an amazing thing.

Blessed are we as we sit and ponder.

Blessed to feel all that is offered.

- - - - - -

Tuesday 1st January 2013 - 5:30 pm

It's different now.

I still love you, I still miss you, I still feel you.

But it's different now.

How could I have known 2 years ago that this was going to happen?

But it's different now.

We danced into the new year as our lives unfolded.

But it's different now.

Time together, time away, then together again.

But it's different now.

Then in the moment we danced again and then you were gone.

It's different now.

Jude

With Love

- - - - - -

Friday 18th January 2013

Write my way out of a slump – how on earth do I do that when I feel so stuck on planet earth that I can't find my way home?

Where's home? It's a place where I feel so alone. Let's see where we can go from here. Take a day ... take a moment to be with me. Let's have some time with my camera and me.

A story in pictures. A moment to be. Touches of spirit. A touch of me. To let it all happen is to let my tune play so beautifully.

May I open my heart to the beauty I see and make it all happen for me and for them. To take the first step just pick up your camera and make a start. It's easy.

Please do it for me ... please do it for me. It all will unfold right before your eyes. You have it, you can do it and joy will unfold. It's all in your hands ... it's ready to go.

- - - - - - -

Monday 28th January 2013

I'm feeling ...

Life is full of so many feelings, some we like and some we don't. These feelings consciously or unconsciously run our lives.

Practising tuning into your feelings is a great way to live in the moment and enrich your life. Repressed feelings are always there waiting to burst out.

There is a saying: "what you resist persists" so allow your feelings to flow in the spaces provided in this journal. Give yourself permission to have these feelings.

Like the waves in the ocean, feelings come and go when you allow them to be. All feelings have a purpose in assisting your growth.

Start now with: "I'm feeling ... "

- - - - - -

Friday 8th March 2013

Yum - it's great when your kids grow up and you have a choice to go out without them. We headed out for an adventure to somewhere thinking Yarra river/city. The traffic was terrible so we diverted to the left and discovered a Malaysian restaurant in South Yarra. Yum! So delicious we might invite the kids next time.

Wednesday 27th March 2013

Bath

Sea Salts

Mariner

Candle Holder – gift from John

Writing – how – next step

Journals – gift from Mum – too beautiful to use

Value myself

Write – read – lay it out – share it

Friday 19th April 2013

Beautiful one day - perfect the next. Relaxing on my front porch with a cup of chamomile tea. Yesterday I enjoyed the raindrops, today I enjoy the sunshine. Enjoy the beauty that surrounds you wherever you are.

- - - - - - -

Saturday 11th May 2013 - 2:00 pm

"Mum Moments" ☺

Okay, so it's the day before Mother's Day.

Everywhere I go I see mothers and daughters sharing and loving, laughing and smiling together.

Oh boy, I'm still now and I'm feeling it ... feeling the loss, feeling the emotion of not sharing this gorgeous day with my Mum.

Everyone knows that their mum is the best mother in the world, but I know my Mum's the best ever. The one who loves me everyday, all day everyday, through the highs, the lows and in betweens. Whatever happens, whatever she feels, no matter what, she loves me with a passion only mothers know.

Only a mother can know that feeling of love that goes beyond all boundaries, stretches to the end of the world, stretches to the end of time and further than any existence we can possibly know on earth.

I'm sure in the essence of her new world her passion and love for me will live forever.

But today, as another Mother's Day beckons, I miss her smiling face, her physical touch and her being here to share with me and my family the wonder of who she is.

My Mum ☺

I love you Mum.

xoxoxo

- - - - - -

Monday 13th May 2013 - 8:30 am

The Blah Blah Blah

The journey continues to change. Death like life has many twists and turns and the more I try to control my feelings or actions around death and what it means the more I discover I can't.

I've come to the realisation that death is just like life.

It's an experience that unfolds in every moment of the day.

It becomes part of your life the moment someone close to you dies.

The reality hits you like a brick wall.

All of a sudden this person ... this person that you took for granted would always be there whenever you both chose to connect and share some space and share some time ... is not there.

- - - - - -

I'm sitting with my "Mum Moments" and I have writer's block.

Writing is something that comes naturally to me when the feelings flow

The feelings flow daily.

What's the next step?

Sometimes I write to her

Sometimes I talk to her

Sometimes I miss her

Sometimes I feel her

Sometimes I ache for her

Sometimes I feel

- - - - - -

Monday 13th May 2013 - 10:40 am

I have just spent some dedicated, peaceful time sitting and connecting with my Mum. Since her death I have found this time to be healing in the grieving process. I feel surrounded by her love ... her presence at these times is truly amazing.

This moment is for me and Mum. Dedicated to just being together for a while.

She may be dead and I'm alive, however the relationship we have known in life still continues, even in death.

I know, she knows what we shared. We are the only ones who really know the depths of our relationship ... the connection, the bond and the undying love between mother and child.

When I am still in any moment there is always something surrounding me that touches me, reminds me of her.

When she was alive I'm not sure I recognised how powerful our relationship was, but now she is dead I know that we have the power to make a difference ... to love and be loved, to change directions and change the directions of others for the benefit of our highest good.

As I sit and ponder, feeling the warmth of the heater, the thought comes: "Touched by an Angel". Once she was an "Angel on Earth" and now she is an "Angel in Heaven".

I hope everyone who experienced her touch in life can still feel her touch in death. It is a powerful touch that transcends life and death. Oh, how beautiful it is to experience her touch.

I love you Mum.

Jude

Everyday is a Mother's Day. ☺

- - - - - - -

Monday 13th May 2013 - later

Some of the ways I connect with Mum, share time with her, feel her.

- Her shawl
- Her friends
- Favourite shops
- Favourite places
- Walking
- Nelson Bay – beach walks – dedicated times
- Photos
- Her quirks
- Latte with jug of milk
- Marcello – flowers
- Her grave occasionally … however she's everywhere
- The ocean
- Cup of Tea

Some of the ways she connects with me

- "Cross the road Jude" – her voice resonates with me
- "Cup of tea with me" – leads to Allison DuBois book
- Clear instructions
- Ring mum feeling
- Reminds me to be in the moment

- Wanting her drum ... "you don't need the drum to be with me"
- She talks to me
- Asking to channel through me
- The thought of her guides me somewhere and often I find something else that is perfect for me right now

- - - - - -

Wednesday 15th May 2013

Sometimes being a parent sucks. Blah blah blah blah blah!

I was hesitant to write this but it's the truth.

Sometimes is a wonderful word.

Sometimes I'm happy, sometimes I'm sad, sometimes everything just seems to fall into place and other times not.

Sometimes parenting is a wonderful experience and sometimes it sucks.

Sometimes you just have to experience the emotion in the moment.

- - - - - -

Monday 20th May 2013 - 10:30 am

Good Morning Mum.

In the silence of the morning as I nurture and care for myself, I am reminded of all that is important for me ... all that resonates.

When I allow my 'Mum Moments' time I am surprised with what unfolds. My intuition kicks in and guides me on a pathway previously unknown, guides me to a place, a space with peaceful outcomes that surprise me.

I am aware of how much time I can spend organising, planning, making sure everything gets done 'just right' - whatever that is - so going with the flow is a wonderful experience that creates peaceful outcomes.

On this wonderful morning I have meditated, soaked in a bath, enjoyed an ongoing cup of chamomile tea, planted some herbs, removed some weeds and given myself precious time for my "Mum Moments".

Whilst I share 'Mum Moments' with you in so many different ways everyday, I have found this dedicated time every week has been a blessing in opening up my own awareness, nurturing myself and being kind to me.

I thank you for all the gifts you have taught me in life and death and beyond.

May our journey together grow deeper and stronger as we continue along our pathways.

With Love

Jude

- - - - - -

Monday 27th May 2013 - 10:20 am

"Take the rush out of it Jude," I hear her say ...

As I take a breath and sip on my tea, I realise I'm' focusing on the destination of my writing rather than the journey.

My journal is precious to me and mostly handwritten as that's how it flows. Paper and pen wherever I am works for me as the words unfold.

Rewriting my words with a keyboard for safekeeping in the computer is a journey of its own and wonderful way to paint the canvas of my experience.

My vision is to share my experience through a published journal that helps others to connect with their own personal journey.

This book will provide some space for others to write, to feel, to be in touch with what's happening for them in any given moment.

My hope is that others can find a place of peace through this journey of life and death and the grief that unfolds.

- - - - - -

Tuesday 4th June 2013

Awareness is the key - acknowledge the feelings you are sensing - be kind to every feeling as each one has a purpose. Get to know these feelings and understand their purpose so you can choose how you react when the feeling presents.

- - - - - -

Saturday 20th July 2013

Awareness - we all need to take responsibility for our own awareness.

- - - - - -

Monday 22nd July 2013 - 11:00 am

It's the little things

The precious moments

The time alone

The time together

The thoughts that flow

The heart that's broken

And then you know

It's the little things that bring you Joy.

It's the little things

The stories told

The stories shared

The time to laugh

The time to cry

The time to be together

The time to be alone

It's the little things

It's the little things

The cup of tea

The taste of food

The taste of life

The smell of life

The precious gifts

It's the little things

- - - - - -

Saturday 27th July 2013 – early morning

A mothers love, dedication and commitment are forever.

- - - - - -

10:30 am

Be there – say little.

- - - - - -

Sunday 28th July 2013

Woohoo, I'm editing my journal.

Wow what a journey.

Living in the moment my writing flows and I love it. My greatest challenge in taking my writing to a new level and publishing my journal is me. I'm consciously practising removing the blockages I have created. The experience is enlightening.

- - - - - -

Thursday 1st August 2013

The Flu has engulfed my whole being this week. I am so sick and feeling vulnerable. I'm finding it difficult to be in the moment! In the middle of the night I just wanted my Mum to take care of me, to cook me some of her chicken soup. It's times like this I really miss her physical presence in my life. Mothers have an amazing capacity to nurture their children when they are sick. xoxoxo

- - - - - -

Sunday 11th August 2013 - 1:30 pm

Contentment - I can learn a lot from our dog Tye. Find a patch of sunshine and soak it up!

- - - - - -

Sunday 11th August 2013 - 3:30 pm

Sometimes I find life overwhelming and sometimes I resist the feeling and the overwhelm takes over. When I embrace the feeling without judgment and allow it to present it passes. All feelings have a purpose - when I let them flow my life flows too. I love writing - it's a powerful healing tool for me. I am enjoying the sunshine today. I hope you are experiencing sunshine too. ☺

- - - - - -

Tuesday 3rd September 2013 - 9:20 pm

Losing my Mum was one of the most devastating things ever to happen to me.

She was my rock through the most difficult times in my life.

Oh how I miss her. Oh how I long for her.

The emotion is overwhelming at times. It takes me completely by surprise.

Thank God for writing ☺

- - - - - -

Tuesday 10th September 2013 - 11:37 am

Up close and honest.

Real self expression that makes people say yes I can relate to that.

As I sit and ponder I had the epiphany that my "Mum Moments" journal is ready to go out into the big wide world and I'm excited. I'm excited for me and I'm excited for all the people that are going to read it. I know it has assisted me on my journey since Mum's death and I know it will assist others as they take their own journey through death and grieving.

I am so happy that I have written this for me, shared it with and for my Mum, and will be sharing it with others who take comfort in self expression.

Who would have thought that I would find my shining light through the loss of my mother? She always knew there was a spark inside of me ready to shine. I hope my shining light is of benefit to all who read my journal.

- - - - - -

Monday 23rd September 2013 - 10:54 am

Springtime – yellow daisies in the park – warm sunshine brings a smile to my face as I remember my Mum and my childhood. ☺

- - - - - -

I love you Mum

- - - - - -

Tuesday 18th February 2014 – early morning

As I complete the editing of 'Mum Moments' the words continue to unfold ...

Grief is a journey ... embrace it and it takes you where you need to go in any given moment.

I was awoken in the early hours of this morning. It was time to write as I embrace the reality again that my mother, my soul mate, died three years ago.

This journey will continue, sometimes with the joy of being surrounded by her love in any given moment and sometimes with the pain and reality of the physical loss.

I know I have my writing to guide me through.

- - - - - - -

Tuesday 18th February 2014 - 4:30am

I remember lighting a candle for you as you lay in the ICU at the Alfred Hospital ... something to stay connected as I came to terms with letting you go.

At the time it made sense. Spiritually you were ready to go and I embraced the knowing that this was meant to be.

This was your time.

I never knew just how much pain I would experience in letting you go from this physical world. I never knew how many times I would ache for you, cry for you, miss you and just feel it's so damn unfair. I want you back ... I want you here in this world, the one I live in ... not on the spiritual path.

I miss you so much.

It is 3 years on the 20th February since you died and it still hurts. I miss you and I want you here with me. I want to love you. I want to cuddle you. I want my mum.

I want to share my journal with you. I want to share my survival technique for living through your death.

I am so proud to be your daughter and so grateful.

I love you with my heart and soul.

Jude xoxoxo

- - - - - - - - -

4:57 am

As I sit quietly in the early hours with the light of a burning candle, I realise your light continues to shine in my life.

I miss you Mum.

Love Jude xoxoxo

- - - - - - - - -

5:00 am

The power of love ...

There are no words ...

It just is ....

Tuesday 18th February 2014 - 5:09 am

As the tears flow I still find it hard to believe she's not here. She feels so alive to me that it makes no sense.

- - - - - - - - -

5:12 am

A peace and serenity surrounds me as I sit quietly in bed with my Mum's shawl wrapped around my shoulders.

She's with me. It's different now.

I love you Mum.

- - - - - - - - -

5:15 am

Sleep beckons as I feel the warmth of my Mum ... here with me, cuddling me, supporting me, loving me as she did when I was a child.

I am surrounded by her love always.

Jude xoxoxo

Thank you.

There are so many people I would like to thank for their contribution to Mum Moments.

I am grateful to each and every person who has contributed to the completion of my journal.

You know who you are and I send you a message of love and appreciation for being part of my journey.

Know in your heart you have contributed and I am forever grateful for your presence in my life.

Jude xxxooo

March 2014

YOUR MUM MOMENTS

Mothers give us the gift of life and then our journey begins.

They play an important part in our life with both positive and negative influences.

This is your personal space to record your feelings about your own "Mum Moments" and the influences your Mother has on your life.

I found when I wrote my "Mum Moments" it really helped me deal with my feelings.

It was through writing this journal that I was able to truly connect with my own personal experience with my Mum.

Start now with: "Who is your Mum?"

www.ingramcontent.com/pod-product-compliance
Lightning Source LLC
Chambersburg PA
CBHW072048290426
44110CB00014B/1596